A Torn Heart of Love

What NOT To Do With Your Life!

Mary Kuehn

Glorified Publishing
PO Box 8004
The Woodlands, TX 77387
www.GlorifiedPublishing.com

Dedication

First, I want to dedicate this book to the Lord Jesus Christ who has forgiven me all my sins, washed me clean in his blood and given me the gift of eternal life.

Second, to all the young women that this story of my life will have an impact on, to not make the same mistakes I made.

Lastly, to all my family and friends. Each one of you has a special place in my heart and you have loved me unconditionally. I love each one of you and I thank the Lord for all of you.

.

ENDORSEMENTS

This is a heartfelt story of choices, consequences, and the goodness of God. A wonderful story that proves no matter where you are, God will turn things around and complete the story He has for you. A must read for anyone that thinks they have gotten off track and God will never be able to use them. We are so blessed to have Mary in our church family. She is a mighty woman of God with a strong anointing. We know her story will inspire you and give you hope. Jeremiah 29:11

~Warriors Worship Center Church
Pastor Michael & Jamie Constantine

Mary Kuehn is a personal friend of mine, we have known each other for the last 35 years. I have seen her grown from a babe is Christ to a mature woman of God. We have spent many hours together studying and learning about the word of God, his Kingdom and of our Saviour Jesus Christ. Through the years Mary has always loved to share the things she has learned and is always eager to help others learn. She always points people to Jesus Christ.

A friend forever,
Jeanette Russo

Mary Kuehn, a personal friend, exposes the deepest secrets of her life for all to read. Secrets she reveals even her own family and friends were not aware of. She shares her most hidden experiences in detail. Mary had to make one of the most heart breaking decisions any mother would ever have to make. This book will impact and benefit a heart of any age. After becoming a Christian, the keys she shares are very powerful. Allow the Lord to

Mary Kuehn

set you free from shame and guilt. He will guide you from going down the wrong paths.

Evangelist Marie Owens
The Master's Touch Ministries
Formally Preacher Lady 1140 KYOK

CONTENTS

Mary Kuehn

ACKNOWLEDGMENTS

I would like to acknowledge my best friend and spiritual mother Jeanette Russo. Thank you from the bottom of my heart for all the years you have invested in me. I know the Lord must have an awesome crown for all your sacrifices you have made on my behalf. You have been God's mouth piece that has spoken into my life countless times over the last thirty-three years.

I would also like to thank Edie Bayer, for all her time and work on helping me and giving me the encouraging words to complete this story of my life.

Mary Kuehn

DISCLAIMER

The names of most of the people who I talk about in my book have been changed. Some are now deceased.

The events in this book, described here as my life story, are true. Other people may remember these events differently, but these are my memories, and this is how I remember them.

Mary Kuehn

INTRODUCTION

The Lord spoke to me two different times that I was to share my life story with people. He said that it would help many young girls. It is out of obedience that you are reading this account.

A lot of good has happened in my life, and I have made good decisions, but I have also made some bad mistakes. What I am writing about in this book are the effects on my life, and what these decisions and mistakes cost me, either way.

There are things that I chose to do, even when I knew better. In addition, I was told by some of my family members that I was making a mistake, and they urged me not to go through with my plans.

I should have listened, that I know now. I also know that those days can never be re-lived. I can never reach back into my past, and try to redo what I did then. If I would have taken to heart what they were trying to tell me, my life story would be completely different.

You will probably want to judge me, either good or bad, that is your choice. I can only thank the Lord that my past sins are forgiven and I no longer have to bear the weight of them anymore. As I share my life' experiences with you, it is my prayer that what I did back then will help you now, both today, and in your future.

Mary Kuehn

Mary Kuehn

Chapter 1

My story begins in 1946, on the 20th of September. I was born about a year after my parents married. My Dad was a Sergeant in the U.S. Army. After he was discharged, he and my Mom were married in Bryan, Texas. You see, that's where most of my family came from. Being born in 1946, I am what you would call a 'baby boomer'. That's what children who were born during that time were called. You see that's because all the men, and a lot of women, came home from serving in the army, navy or whatever they had served in during the second world war. That's why so many babies were born in and around the early and middle 1940's.

My grandparents came to the U.S.A. from Sicily in the early 1900's. In fact, both sets of my great grandparents came to the U.S.A. on boats from there. I often wonder what they felt after leaving their homes, and all the people they knew there, and coming here to America. I don't know why, but they never talked about their past lives from the old country. I can only think their lives had to be very hard.

My Mom's and Dad's parents all knew each other, as well as other Italian families, so back in those days here in the U.S.A. it wasn't unusual for Italians to marry other Italians. They all had the same beliefs, as well as traditions, whereas Americans' beliefs were not quite the same.

My parents lived in Houston after their marriage, so that's where I grew up, as well as my younger brother and sister. My Dad's parents and all his sisters and brothers lived in Bryan, but soon made the move to Houston. They all pretty much lived in the same neighborhood, but my Mom's family still lived in Bryan as farmers, raising cotton and corn.

As was the custom for Italians to raise their families, I was baptized Catholic as a baby, made my first communion and also made my confirmation. I remember burning candles in the church and going to vacation Bible school. I was taught the rosary, going to the Catholic priest for confession, and attending and being a part of the traditional St. Joseph table that was a yearly Sicilian custom. Being raised a Catholic is where I learned about Jesus, the cross, and how to worship God. I knew of God, but really didn't have a true relationship with Him. I thank God for allowing me to learn to believe in Jesus, and what he did on the cross at Calvary.

My Mom was an everyday housewife, and stayed home to raise the family and did her daily chores of cooking and cleaning. She taught us kids not to lie, and to do the best we could. My Dad went to work every day to support us. That is just how things were in those days. Nowadays it takes both parents to provide for the family.

Of course, as time went on, as a young girl I began to mature early, which most Italian girls do. In fact, it was to such a point that when I was in the fourth grade, the teacher I had in elementary school was a bit jealous of my breasts that were starting to form. You are probably thinking that I am exaggerating, but I am not. I was already wearing a training bra. I don't remember her name anymore. I am sure she is probably deceased by now. She was already up in age back then.

In those days, we didn't have a television, so I used to sit on my Mom's kitchen cabinet and listen to the radio.

I remember as a young girl, in about the fifth grade, I met this special girl one day as we were walking to school. We became friends right off the bat. Her name was Susan, and we had a really great friendship. We did everything together. We walked to school together every day, spent the night at each other's house, and went to school sock hops together. In those days, songs like Blue Velvet, Splish Splash, The Twist and many more were the songs that we loved, and were popular. That's when Elvis Presley was just beginning his career. It was the age of rock and roll.

We went to school football banquets together with our dates. We played in the school band together. We both played the clarinet.

I wanted to learn to play the drums, but my Mom said no that was for boys. We went to the show every Saturday with our friends. We all went swimming together. Susan and I became as close as any two sisters could ever be.

I remember hiding from our parents and smoking cigarettes. One particular day I was smoking in Susan's room, when unexpectedly her Mom came home! I threw the lit cigarette in her waste basket. I just knew I was going to catch the house on fire. Thank goodness nothing happened!

We made a blood covenant between ourselves. We both scratched our wrists and put them together. We didn't know the importance of what we were doing at that time. Here we are some fifty-something years later, and we are still in contact with each other, and still close friends.

Back in those days, we were so close when we were in junior high school, that we even began to have our monthly periods at the same time. I don't know how that happened, but it did.

Growing up in the early 1950's, those were the good ole days. We wore bobby socks with our penny loafers. We wore about three starched petty coats under our skirts so that they looked really full. We also wore black and white oxford shoes that we had to always keep polished.

In those days we rode our bikes everywhere we went, or else we had to walk a lot to get where we wanted to go. We went dancing on

Saturday nights sometimes at a local park. We still talk about those days.

I remember one night during the winter, Susan was spending the night at my house, and my Dad was at work. We decided to crawl out of the window and go to her house. It was so cold, and we were going down the drive way on our hands and knees, and we got to giggling. If I remember right, Mom had her window cracked a little and caught us. I don't think we did that again!

A lot of Saturdays we rode the city bus downtown and went shopping. We didn't have much money but we still had a great time. In those days we had attic fans, slept with all the windows open during the summer nights and we never felt fear. We played outside until it was dark. Things were a lot different in those days, compared to now.

Mom and Dad had what we called an "ice box". I remember the ice man coming by our house in his truck to deliver a block of ice every other day. I remember the day that my Dad came home with an air conditioner. It was heavenly!

After school, a lot of days, Susan and I would get together on my Mom's and Dad's front porch. They had a swing and we would just sit out there and talk, and laugh about what happened at school that day, or something that one of our friends did.

It wasn't long before some of the boys we went to school with would come over on their bikes. They would be parked all over

Mom's and Dad's front yard. Sometimes my Dad would come home from work, and would get really hacked because of all the guys that were hanging around, and tell me that they had to go. I really hated that. There wasn't anything bad going on; in fact, we were all just good friends. Sometimes we would hang out at Susan's house.

I have so many good memories from my childhood. I had a lot of really good aunts, uncles and cousins, as I have mentioned before. In the summer time, I used to spend time with some of my family in Bryan, and visit with cousins my age. As I said, my grandparents still lived there, and were still farmers.

I remember my Grandma, my Mom's mother, would get outside and plant her own vegetable garden. She was really up in age, but that sure never stopped her. My grandparents couldn't speak much English, but did know a little, enough that we could understand each other. I always wanted to learn to speak Italian, but never did.

I had another aunt that was one of my favorites. Aunt Mae was married to one of my Dad's brothers. She and my cousin Ann lived in Houston as well. I spent many a weekend with them. A lot of weekends they would go to the Gulf Coast. Her family lived in a small town close to Bay City.

I love the memories of those days. We would go and camp on the beach at night, build camp fires and my Dad and the other family members would go floundering at night with a light and a gig. We would go crabbing and fishing, too. The moon and the stars were so awesome in the night sky and you could hear the waves washing up to the shore line. Many times I longed to relive those wonderful days. My life was so innocent and simple in those days of years gone by.

Chapter 2

When I was about 14 years old, my life changed, and it wasn't for my good, although at that time I just didn't realize it. I was spending a weekend at my Aunts Mae's house with my cousin Ann. My cousin Ann had made new friends with a girl named Cynthia that lived on the back street.

Her brother, Donny, had just gotten home from the Navy. I think his parents had gotten him home on a hardship case, if my memory is right. Regardless, I was introduced to him. I remember the day like it was yesterday.

That's the day when things started to change. Donny had asked me if I could go out on a date. At that time, my Dad didn't allow me to go out, but I managed to talk him into it. As time went on, we were dating and one thing led to another. I just knew I was so in love with him.

We began going steady, and as time went by we began to talk of marriage. At that time I was fourteen, and he was nineteen. As I look back to those days, I now realize it was nothing but a bad case of puppy love. How could any fourteen year old child know what real love could ever be? Nobody could tell me any different. I was so headstrong.

Here I was, in the eighth grade in junior high school, and getting ready to make one of the biggest mistakes of my life. All of my school friends had kind of drifted off, because I was so involved with this older guy. One day, I even asked one of them why she didn't come around anymore. The answer I got was, "Well, you are hanging around with this older guy so much."

Why I didn't stop and think about what I was missing out on, I don't know. Sometimes I think, that maybe if they had come around at that time, things would have worked out differently for me, but that's just my thinking. These were my choices.

As time went on and we had been dating for a good while, he asked me if I would go to bed with him. Without counting the cost, I gave up my virginity. What an awesome mistake I made. If I could relive those days, I would have thought twice, but I felt so in love with him and I thought he really loved me. If anyone is reading my story please don't make this same mistake I did. You see, after a few months I came up pregnant. I was so afraid to tell my parents.

I was really praying so hard and seeking God to help me and I immediately started my period.

I know for sure that I received a true miracle from the Lord that day. And I will never believe any different.

I should have broken off the engagement then, that the Lord was giving me a way of escape. But, oh no! I just kept on going, doing what I wanted to do. I just kept on the wrong path for my life. If anyone was to ask me why I didn't make a change then I honestly couldn't give them an answer. The only possible one would be that I thought I was in love with this person.

The Lord was giving me the way of escape, but I made the choice to keep on the wrong path for my life. You see, from the time you are born, God has a plan and a destiny for your life. Our mistakes, or decisions, can change our whole destiny.

Things finally ended up that I had to tell my parents that we decided to go ahead and get married a little sooner than planned. I didn't tell them that I was now pregnant, but sometimes I think that they probably had an idea of what was going on.

My Dad and I went up to the Junior High School to talk to the principal, to tell him that I was quitting school and getting married. The principal told me, "Don't you know you have the grades to go to college on?" I acted as if I didn't care. So my Dad signed the papers, and I was no longer a student.

Here I was, fourteen years old, had just quit school, pregnant and making plans on a wedding. We ended up going to the court house in Houston and getting married before a judge. That night we had a small celebration at my parents' house with all the family and friends over. Mom and Dad served sandwiches, chips, snacks and a nice wedding cake.

We did get a lot of nice gifts that night. As we were leaving our wedding reception, we took off running, and had to jump the ditch in front of my parents' house to get to our car. Well, wouldn't you know it, I fell right in the ditch in front of everyone. I got up, extremely embarrassed, got in the car and we left. Now, you would have thought that with some of the money we got from the wedding gifts, we would have gotten a nice hotel room for the night. It appeared that it didn't mean that much to him. Beyond my wildest dreams, he drove us to his grandparents' house and that's where we spent our first married night together, with them in the next room.

The next day, my Dad and Donny's Dad got together and bought furniture, and helped us to move into a nice little house we had rented in the Heights area. Well, of course when he came home, all he had to do was just walk in. Everything was in place and unpacked. So began our married life.

By that time, I was having a lot of morning sickness. I was sick every time I ate. By now, both of our parents knew I was expecting.

Soon after we were married, he got to where he wasn't coming home at night. I didn't have a television, only a radio and some books. That is how I filled my days, sitting on my new couch, day after day, alone. His parents would come to get me some days, and I would spend time with them until he got home. Then it would all start over again. I have to say his parents were always so good to me. They are both deceased now.

At night, I was afraid of every little noise. Finally, after a little while later, he came to me and said he needed some time to think about this marriage, and suggested I go back home to my parents. I knew then that was going to be the end. This was his excuse to get me to leave. I knew there was no use in saying no to him, so I contacted my family and his, and they all came over to help me pack up and move. I was so young and immature back then. I should have been going to school. I would never know what it would be like to walk across a platform, to get to graduate from high school, with my friends. I would never know what I could have had in my future.

When all our friends and family found out we were going to split up, some of his family members even asked for their wedding gifts back. I gave them to them, but I really didn't have to. I figured, what's the use, anyway?

At this point, I was now moving back home, with no education, no money, I couldn't drive and expecting a baby. Why did I allow myself to get into such a horrible mess? Only God knows how stubborn I was, and just wouldn't listen to people who really cared about me enough to tell me the truth. I was way too young to even think about marriage, but I wouldn't listen to anybody.

Sometimes my husband would give me some money, but not very often. I remember all the nights I cried, and told my baby, "That's ok, I am here for you, and I will take care of you."

As time went on, he asked me if we could get back together, which I was in full agreement of doing. But it ended up that things went right back to the same old story. So, what did I do? I went right back to my parents' house. The truth of the matter is we were both too young. The old saying is, *if you play with fire you can be sure you just might get burned.* We never did reconcile after that.

I lived with my parents from then on. I had hired a lawyer and filed for divorce. I needed money from him to buy things for the baby and for myself. I did end up with a baby shower, so that really helped out a lot.

I was going to a doctor in the Heights area for my pregnancy. He was great, and he knew all about my story. The day that I went to give birth, I had promised his parents that I would call and let them know, which I did. They came up to the hospital to see me. My husband came up, also. Things did not go well, as I remember. He told me that the baby was not his. I think he did that out of fear of having the responsibilities.

I was so hurt, all I could do was just cry. Soon after my husband left the room, my doctor came in to check on me, and found me crying. He asked what was wrong. I told him. He left the room and gave orders to the nurses that my husband was not allowed back in the hospital. I will never forget the look of sadness that my doctor had on his face, as I laid in the hospital bed. I was a child having a child.

My baby daughter was born on November 21st, 1961, at 1:52 p.m. You couldn't have asked for a more beautiful and healthy baby. My Dad was at the hospital with me when she was born. Thank God for my Dad! When my three days was up, he came and picked me and my baby girl up to take us home. My Mom was home taking care of my brother and sister, who were still very young.

You see, whatever choices we make, there will be a consequence to pay, either good or bad. You might be saying, well, maybe a lot of what I went through was not my fault. Yes, that may be true of some of it, but the bottom line is, I didn't value my life, or my future, enough to stop and think what I was really getting myself into. Life is short, and life is what you make it. I have just shared one part of my life's story, and oh, there is so much more for me to tell.

Mary Kuehn

Chapter 3

Eventually, my Mom and Dad moved, and bought a grocery store. My Dad continued to work for the city and my Mom ran the store. When the store got really busy with customers, I would help her out.

My Dad used to buy grocery supplies at one of the local grocery wholesale dealers on his off day to restock the store. He met a young man named Gene that worked there and they became good friends. Soon, he started coming to the store to deliver the groceries to my parents. I was introduced to Gene. He appeared to be a very nice kind of guy, or so I thought.

Gene was immediately attracted to me, and me to him. By then my divorce was final, and he asked me for a date. We did date for a good while. He really seemed to care a lot for me and my baby girl. He just seemed to be a really good, perfect person. As time went on, needless to say, eventually he asked me to marry him. He said that he loved me, and my baby girl, and wanted to take care of us.

What a joke that turned out to be.

My parents thought highly of him, and my baby girl was really attached to him. Things seemed to be going so good. Even my other family members thought he was great.

Well, for about a year we lived in a garage apartment close to my parents and all my other family. Things really were going so good. But, it wasn't long before that changed, too.

He had an aunt and uncle who lived in Houston. They had a house that they owned, and were moving. They had offered us the house, a really nice brick house on about an acre of land. We were supposed to rent-to-own it. So we said yes, that was great, and moved.

Things soon began to change. You see, he had lived with them there before we had met. All of his old friends as well as girlfriends still lived in that area, unbeknownst to me. I never even thought anything about that, until it was too late.

Before long I was spending days and nights by myself with my baby girl in the house. Oh, he made sure I had groceries, but no time with him. He would come home in the evening, want to make love, clean up and leave. I wouldn't see him again till the next afternoon. I don't know where he went or what he was doing. But, in fact, one day in the yard by the garbage can the wind had blown a piece of paper in the yard. I found a ticket he had gotten on the Galveston causeway. I asked him if he was with another woman.

A Torn Heart of Love: What NOT to Do with Your Life!

He didn't deny it, as if things weren't already bad enough. I was so hurt. Here we go again, another bad marriage. I already had my baby girl, and now I was pregnant with my second baby. I had found out I was expecting right after we moved there. My Dad kept telling me to hang in there, that when I had my baby, he might change.

Oh God, not again! This just can't be happening to me again. What is becoming of my life?

I tried, I really tried. I didn't want to have to go through another divorce again, especially now when I would have two babies.

I remember right before we made the move to his Aunt and Uncles house, we had made a trip to his Mom's house, who lived in another state. His sister and her family as well as one of his uncles lived there. On the trip down there, he told me do not tell them you are going to have a baby.

I didn't know why he had told me that then. Now, as I look back I can see why. He already knew what was in his heart... he already had made his plans.

When we got to his mother's house, she was so happy to meet me and my baby. We took to her immediately. After a few days of our visit, his Mom and sister asked when we were going to think about adding to our family. I didn't want to lie so I told them I was expecting. They were so happy and excited.

When I told him what had happened, he said I told you not

to tell them. As I said, it wasn't long before I began to know why. I couldn't believe this was happening to me again.

I had made friends with a couple who lived on our street, Jenny and Dave. They had been good friends with his aunt and uncle. If it wasn't for my friendship with them, especially her, I think I would have lost my mind. After we made friends, my baby daughter and I spent many afternoons with her. She was very special to me, both she and her husband.

They knew what was going on, so I think that's why she kind of took me under her wing. She treated me like a daughter. She and her husband had wanted to have a baby so badly, but couldn't. In a lot of ways, she became like a second mother to me.

Again, this is where my life began to take another turn, and not for my good. Let me say this, my friend, sometimes people will make decisions they never thought they would have to face. If you have ever found yourself in a situation like I have, or maybe even close to it, you may be faced with the unthinkable. That's why we should never try to judge someone for the decisions, or actions, that they may have to make.

No one really knows what's going on in that person's life, but them. You won't know the hurts, or trauma, or the stress that they may have had to endure, much less the loneliness or the mistreatment that they may have had to try to live with.

An abortion would have been an easy way out for me; no

responsibility of having to raise two kids without a husband. I understand that sometimes in our lives we are faced with a decision that is almost too much to bear. If, in your past, you did decide to have an abortion, know that the baby is in heaven with the Lord. The Bible says that to be absent from the body is to be present with the Lord.

Know that the Lord loves you! He does not love the sin in our lives, but he still loves us, regardless. Just ask for forgiveness. The Bible says he is faithful, and just to forgive.

You are probably thinking, there is no way God can forgive me. I have made too many mistakes in my life. Oh yes, He does, I can guarantee you that from my firsthand experience. When you give your life to the Lord, you no longer have to carry the guilt, the anger, the fear, the hurts, the regrets and the shame - for you are totally forgiven.

So release yourself from all the bad feeling you are carrying around in your heart and know that God is a God of a second chance.

Don't let abortion be an option. That life is given by God. If you can't make it, like I couldn't, consider adoption. Give that precious life sent from above a chance to live.

As you will see, that is what happened to me. I knew my parents really didn't want me to come back home with another divorce and 2 small babies. I had a small sister, and a handicapped brother at home that my parents were still raising.

I knew it was just a matter of time before my husband would want completely out of the marriage, expecting a new baby or not. I really began to realize that all too soon. I really didn't want to accept the reality of this happening to me again. No, not now, not with my two babies. What was I going to do?

I made a decision that if anyone would have ever told me that I was going to make, I would have told them they were completely out of their minds.

I am sure that there will be very few of you who could ever understand what I am about to share, but that's ok. The Lord knows: what I did, I did out of pure love for my babies.

You see, I knew I was not able to support both of my babies on my own. Here I was, just seventeen years old. Are you surprised? No car, no job, no education, no real home of my own to care for them. Facing a second divorce, when most kids my age were nowhere even close to a situation where I now found myself. Heaven knows, they were still in high school, enjoying being with all their friends, and no responsibilies, except turning in home work, getting close to graduation and looking forward to a great future.

All I wanted was to keep my family together, but I knew there was no way. I also knew my precious friend, who had helped make my life bearable, wanted desperately to have a baby of her own.

So, in the best interest of my unborn baby, I called my Dad and told him I was considering giving my baby up for adoption to her. He was in agreement, and we decided it would be best for me and my baby girl to go ahead, and come back home and try to make it, for which I was grateful.

When my husband came home that evening, I asked him if we could talk, and he said yes. Of course, he was completely overjoyed with us giving away our baby. In fact, he was a little too happy, if you ask me.

I remember telling him, "Why didn't you just leave me alone? Why have you ruined my life?" He gave me no answer. He knew what I was saying was true.

Most people would be saying, "How could you, your husband, your Mom and Dad make such an awful decision -- to give up your own flesh and blood?"

I never said it was easy. In fact, it was one of the hardest things I have ever done. I went to my friend, Jenny, and asked her if she would want to take my baby for her and her husband to adopt, and to raise.

She immediately said yes, with no hesitation, so it was decided then and there, that day, this is what we would do. I knew she and her husband could give my baby a life - things that I would never be able to do. They were quite well off. My husband never looked back with second thoughts of what we were doing.

Soon afterward, I made the move back home to my parents'. My Dad got one of his brothers to come and help pack me up, to move me and my little girl back home.

When my time of delivery got closer, my friend Jenny came and picked me up, and I spent the last part of my time staying with them. She and her husband were so good to me. They always showed me love. They made sure I had clothes to wear, took me to the doctor for my checkups, and took me to my Mom and Dads to see my daughter.

The day finally arrived on Thanksgiving of 1963 I began to have signs of going into early labor. We called the doctor and I was told I better get to the hospital as soon as possible. I was soon delivering my baby, a little boy. I asked for my friend, Jenny, all the way through my labor, but they had gone to get something to eat for Thanksgiving dinner.

After I gave birth I told my nurse that I wanted to see my baby. She kept telling me it was better if didn't. I finally stopped asking because I knew it was for the best, even though my heart hurt to hold my precious baby boy.

The next day Jenny brought my Mom up to the hospital to see me. Mom never saw the baby either. While they were in my room, I told my Mom I had to go to the bathroom. That's when I told her I had to be sure before I could sign the papers giving up my baby; that if there was any chance my marriage might still work, I needed to try.

When I came out of the bathroom I told Jenny what I felt. I knew at once she was hurt, through and through. This was the last thing she would have ever wanted to hear. I could see the hurt in her face. After a while she took my Mom home.

That afternoon, I received a call from my husband. With no hesitation, he told me that there was no way of any reconciliation for us, and that he wanted to give up the baby, with no second thoughts. What could I do but accept that as a final answer? I knew then, for sure, I would have to sign the papers giving up my precious baby boy.

I know that this might sound so heartless, but until you are face to face with a situation like I was, and reality hits you in the face - you know that there is no other choice but to do what is best for your baby.

That evening I called Jenny's house. Her husband Dave answered the phone. I had asked to speak to her but he said she wasn't able to talk right then. I knew exactly why: she was so torn up with what had happened at the hospital.

I told him that I had to be sure before I signed the papers. He said he understood. He had children from his first marriage. They had made the phone call to my husband, telling him I needed to know for sure before I signed the papers. As I said, he didn't hesitate in letting me know he had no interest in trying to save the marriage, much less any concern for the baby.

As I remember things, I believe he was quite relieved to be totally free from all responsibilities. I called Jenny and Dave back and told her husband I would be signing the papers in the morning. Very promptly, early that next morning, the attorneys came to the hospital room, where I signed the papers.

I gave up all legal rights to my precious son's life. My only consolation, was in knowing that he would be very well taken care of, and have more of a chance at life than I could ever give him.

Through the years, this couple and I remained close friends. We stayed in contact until my son was grown; in fact, I was even invited to his graduation from high school. He knew who I was, and was always pleasant to me. When he was married, Jenny and Dave sent me a wedding picture of him and his new wife.

My friends are now both deceased. We always had love for one another. I know for a fact that they both loved me as a daughter to themselves.

I visited them both at their home several times, and spent several days with them each time. I remember one particular time they even wanted me to stay an extra day.

So you see now, what I did, I did out of love for my son; however, it was my love for this special couple that the Lord put there for me, that helped me to do this.

A Torn Heart of Love: What NOT to Do with Your Life!

In many ways I was so blessed. Many people who have made the choice to give up their babies don't have the benefits I was allowed.

I will be forever grateful to them for their love for me and for my son, whom they took as their very own, and loved him so much, until their dying day. They gave him their all, in love, and in so many other ways.

Some of what I have shared with you about my life is because of choices I made. Some I had no control over, but still had to suffer the consequences of it. So use your life wisely, as you will always have to live with things, good or bad.

I sometimes think of them, and of all my family members that have gone on. It brings a certain sadness to me. I always loved my family. Please allow me to encourage you to hold your family members close to you. There is nothing as special in anyone's life as their family is. I know all are not perfect, but really, who is?

Mary Kuehn

Chapter 4

What I am now about to share with you, is a part of my life that I am truly not very proud. The choices I made were because of what I had gone through in the past. These events left me totally against men in some of my feelings, and in some respects, hating them. I just wanted to get what I could get out of them. I was so hurt, and felt so rejected, that I just wanted to hurt back.

So here I went, on to more bad choices, and don't think in the end it still didn't cost me. It did.

I guess you can say this is the "X-Rated" part of my life. I have only myself to blame, and no one else. I am the one who had to pay the consequences for my actions, but at the same time, I ended up hurting the ones I loved the most.

After I had gotten my second divorce, and had given up my baby boy, I developed a very bad attitude of wanting to get even, period. I had more than one sexual affair with men. Oh, how dumb I was, thinking I was getting even. I never had a problem with men wanting to date me. Some said I even looked like I could have been a movie star; well, that remains to be unseen now.

I even dated a couple of married men, and had sex with one. As I look back now to those days, I didn't have an ounce of good sense, and I knew better! I had just gone through the same terrible experiences with my own marriages, but now, I was out to hurt others. Please don't allow yourself to go down the same road I did! It's not too late for you.

When you have sex with a man, or a man has sex with a woman, you develop what is called soul ties. God made sex to be part of the marriage covenant, between the man and his wife, and for the two of them *only* in the marriage covenant. The Bible says they become one. Sex is a gift from God for enjoyment in the marriage, and for the couple to reproduce, and have a family.

If a person has sex outside of marriage, s/he needs to break off the soul ties from that affair. Just go before the Lord and confess it. Renounce the soul ties from sex that you have had with any person outside of marriage. Then, declare in the name of Jesus, they are broken off of you.

When I became born again, I had to do that. Before that, I didn't know anything about soul ties. You will be forgiven, and set free.

As time went on, I met my third husband. I fell deeply in

love with him from the very beginning. I have to be completely honest ... I never knew what it was like to really be loved, until I met him.

He had a little boy, and I had my daughter. He was divorced, same as I was, and had custody of his son. Before we married, he asked me one night on one of our dates about my past, if I had ever had sex with other men outside of my two marriages. I looked him straight in the face, and lied.

We went together about a year and half before we married. On June 12th, 1970 I gave birth to our son. My husband had a grin on his face from one side to the other. Now we were a real family: we had his, hers and now, ours.

We raised our children together. They acted as if they were truely brother and sister. In fact, if you didn't know better, you really would have thought they were.

I was beyond being happy. This was something I had never, ever had before in my life. I held this so close to my heart.

From the time I met him in 1966, until about forty one and a half years later, I never told him the truth about my past. I was so ashamed, and didn't want to take a chance on losing this wonderful person, who was as deeply in love with me as I was with him. I never in a million years would have wanted to hurt this man I loved so dearly.

Many nights, I would lay beside him, and just thank God for giving him to me. I never knew what it meant to truly have someone to love me, and treat me and my daughter so well.

He had a new three bedroom house built for us. He always gave me the best. I had just learned what it meant to have a home and a real family. Sure, as a married couple we had our ups and downs as all couples do, but nothing ever serious.

In 2009, which was about forty one and a half years later, things changed in our marriage. By that time, we had raised our family, and had grandchildren.

We were lying in bed one night, and he asked me a question. I don't know to this day if I misunderstood him, or if I had been set up by the enemy.

In 1983, I had become a born again Christian. About a year before that, one of my Dad's brothers came down with stomach cancer. A Christian couple reached out to pray with him and his wife. He accepted the Lord before his death. After that my Aunt stayed close to the Lord, and developed a very deep relationship with him as her Savior.

Around about that same time I was very sick. I had been to my fifth doctor, and third hospital stay. On a Wednesday, she came up to the hospital to see me, and witnessed to me about the Lord. I was having a lot of lung issues, and was on a breathing machine. She talked to me about how the Lord heals people even today, that He paid the price on Calvary's cross for that, as well as for our sins. She asked me if I could believe Jesus to heal me.

I told her yes. That night she was going to church, and was going to get one of the elders to pray in agreement with her for the Lord to heal me. I was home in about two days after that and no longer on breathing machine! The more I believed, the more the symptoms left my body. In a matter of just a few days I was totally healed!

It was at that time, I made the decision to begin going to the non-denominational church that my Aunt was attending. That is where I began to have a relationship with the Lord.

The very first Sunday my family and I attended that church, we met a couple who would forever be in my life in a way I had never known. Talk about a God ordained meeting, this surely was! As a rule, they usually sat up front in the church, but due to a flat tire that morning, they got to the church late and had to sit in the back; in fact, in the pew behind us. They reached out and started talking to us. They were Catholic Italians, and we hit it off first thing. We exchanged phone numbers. As I look back now, that was about thirty three years ago.

That day is when I met Jack and Jeanette. I will be forever grateful to the Lord for allowing our paths to cross. Over the years, we have had such an awesome friendship, totally centered around the Lord Jesus. Jack worked every day, and Jeanette and I began spending a lot of time on the phone. She generously gave of herself to me, teaching me almost daily about my new found faith in the Lord. I can't tell you how many hours she spent with me discipling me, and counselling me, as well.

I pray the Lord would give everyone a special friend, as He has given me. No words can express her kindness to me. If I needed correction, or praise about something, she has always been there for me. Everyone needs a special friend in their life to talk to, and know that things will not go any further.

Over the years we have become more than friends, and are truly sisters in the Lord. Jack has been gone 25 years now, but I will forever be thankful for him coming into my life as well.

You can see now why I didn't want to lie, so I told him the truth of my past. This hit him so hard he actually went to bed totally sick. I cannot tell you how many tears this man shed. I hurt him all the way to his very core. Things were horribly terrible between us after that night. He felt so deceived, his reaction to me was almost more than I could bear, with name calling, throwing all the past up to me, as well as screaming at me out of his hurt.

He felt our whole married life was a lifetime of lies. He even quit wearing his wedding ring. He felt it was a ring of lies and deception. We separated for about two months, and had even filed for divorce. But, because we truly loved each other, that was cancelled and we went back to each other, to try to make our marriage work and be healed.

How many times he told me he wished I had taken all that to my grave when it would be my time. In hindsight, I wish things would have worked out like that myself, but it didn't, so what can I say?

We are now close to seven years down the road. We are still together, and now have great grandbabies. Our marriage has had a lot of healing, and the Lord is still working with us. We both truly love each other, and it's only by the grace of God we are still together. He now wears a new wedding ring. Praise God.

Mary Kuehn

Chapter 5

Don't think the enemy doesn't rise up every so often to do more damage. It is only through the goodness of the Lord that he doesn't win.

I am not telling anybody to go and tell everything about your past life. That's totally up to you. If you feel that the Lord is telling you to do this, pray. Be sure it is the Lord, and not somebody else, or the enemy. I can only share what has happened to me. The Bible says everything that is hidden will be revealed.

By the grace of God, I am what I am. As I look back over the years of my life, I know that the Lord has always been here with me, although I didn't realize it at the time. My life experiences that I have written about are to the very best of my memory, and I feel are totally true. I can only pray that this book will help someone to make better choices for their life, and future.

Since I have given my life over to the Lord, and repented of all my past sins, I have been forgiven. I am the righteousness of Him. My sins are washed away through the blood of Christ, and I am free. My husband is a Christian as well, and we both go to the Lord for help in all areas of our lives.

My husband and I are in leadership over a bible study group that meets on a monthly basis in the Houston area called, "The Gathering". People have been delivered and truly helped. The Lord has allowed me to pray for people, teach His word and minister healing to His people. You see, in God there is no condemnation in Christ Jesus.

The presence of the Lord is truly here. So allow me to leave you with this. Take a step of faith, and trust Jesus with your life. The Bible says no weapon formed against you can prosper. Yes, these things will try to come against you, but God makes a way out.

If you have never given your life to the Lord, please allow me to lead you into a prayer of repentance:

Father, I come to you in the name of Jesus, and I repent of all my sins. Come into my life, and cleanse me with your precious blood that was shed for me on Calvary's cross. In Jesus' name, I pray.

If you have prayed this simple prayer with all of your heart, you are now a child of the living God, and all the angels in heaven are rejoicing as your name is now written in the *Lamb's Book of Life.*

You are now a new creation in Christ Jesus. Start reading God's word and get your mind renewed. Find a good Bible teaching church, and go there. You now have a new and fresh life in Christ. Live for Him. I promise you that you will never regret it.

Mary Kuehn

Chapter 6

SCRIPTURES OF COMFORT

Scriptures for comfort. God's word is true,
and it is life to all who find it.

Ps. 103:10, 12 He has not dealt with us according to our sins, nor punished us according to our iniquities. As far as the east is from the west, so far has He removed our transgressions from us.

II Corinthians 5:17 Therefore, if anyone is in Christ, he is a new creation; old things have passed away; behold all things have become new.

Isaiah 43:25 I, even I, am He who blots out your transgressions for my own sake; and I will forget your sins.

John 15:9, 10 As the Father loved me, I also have loved you; Abide in my love. If you keep my commandments, you will abide in my love, just as I have kept my Father's commandments and abide in His love.

Romans 5:8 But God demonstrates His own love toward us, in that while we still sinners, Christ died for us.

Ps.34:15 The eyes of the Lord are upon the righteous.

Isa. 66:13 As one whom his mother comforts, so will I comfort you

Jer.31:13b For I will turn their mourning into joy, and will comfort them, and make them rejoice rather than sorrow

Ps. 34:10b They that seek the Lord shall not want any good thing.

Ps. 37:4 Delight yourself in the Lord and He shall give you the desires of your heart.

Lk. 12:31 But seek the kingdom of God, and these things shall be added to you.

I Peter 5:7 Casting all your care upon Him; for He cares for you.

Isa 7:11a Ask for a sign for yourself from the Lord your God.

John 14:14 But whoever drinks of water that I shall give him will never thirst. But the water that I shall give him will become in him a fountain of water, springing up into everlasting life.

James 1:6b But let him ask in faith, with no doubting, for he who doubts is like a wave of the sea, driven and tossed by the wind.

James 5:13 Is anyone among you sick? Let him call for the elders of the church, and let them pray over him, anointing him with oil in the name of the Lord.

Jn 15:7 If you abide in me, and my words abide in you, you shall ask what you will and it shall be done for you.

Ps. 34:18 The Lord is near to those who have a broken heart, and saves such as have a contrite spirit.

Isa. 61:3 To console those who mourn in Zion, to give them

beauty for ashes, the oil of joy for mourning, the garment of praise for the spirit of heaviness.

Ps.147:11 The Lord takes pleasure in those who fear Him, in those who hope in His mercy.

Mt.9:29   Then he touched their eyes saying,

"According to your faith let it be to you."

Rom.1:17   For in it the righteousness of God is revealed from faith to faith; as it is written, the just shall live by faith.

Rom.10 17   So then faith cometh by hearing, and hearing by the word of God.

Jeremiah 29:11 For I know the plans I have for you, declares the Lord, plans for welfare and not for evil, to give you a future and a hope.

ABOUT THE AUTHOR

This story is of my life and how I lived because of mistakes I made. I cannot blame anyone but myself.

My family raised me well, but as I got older I decided to do things my way, which did not work out for my good. My family talked to me, but I was too head strong to listen.

Yes, some choices were good, and some not so good, or beneficial to me, and to others. Circumstances were created because of choices I made. These days are in my past and can never be relived.

You will see how I lived my life until I met my third husband. Because of his love for me, I could let go of all the hurt and bitterness I had in my heart. He truly was, and is, a gift given to me from the Lord up above. We have gone through good times and some hard times together these last forty nine years.

The biggest and most important change in my life was when I became a born again Christian. Jesus cleansed me of everything that was not of Him. I started my life all over. The bible says when you ask Jesus in your heart you become a new creation, and are being changed from the inside to the outside.

It is my prayer that you will decide to ask Jesus into your heart and really mean it. I promise you will never be the same.